Frankenstein
Makes a
Sandwich
and Other Stories

You're sure to like,
because they're all
about monsters,
and some of them are
also about food.

"You LIKE FOOD!
Don't You?"

Well, all
right then.

by ADAM REX

MONSTER
SEEKS
BRIDE
SGM SEEKS
GF for friends

Harcourt, Inc.

Orlando   Austin   New York   San Diego   Toronto   London

www.HarcourtBooks.com

An earlier version of
"The Creature from the
Black Lagoon Doesn't Wait
an Hour Before Swimming"
appeared in *Cricket* magazine.

Library of Congress
Cataloging-in-Publication
Data
Rex, Adam.

Frankenstein
makes a sandwich/
Adam Rex.
p. cm.

1. Monsters—Juvenile poetry.   2. Children's poetry, American.   I. Title.
PS3618.E925F73   2006
813'.6—dc22   2005013678
ISBN-13: 978-0-15-205766-4   ISBN-10: 0-15-205766-8

C D E F G H

Manufactured in China

The illustrations in this book were
created with oils and . . . oh gosh,
lots of stuff. What? Sure, he used
some of that. Yep, that, too.
The display type was
created by Adam Rex.
The text type was set in Pastonchi.
Color separations by
Bright Arts Ltd., Hong Kong
Manufactured by South China
Printing Company, Ltd., China
This book was printed on totally
chlorine-free Stora Enso Matte paper.
Production supervision by Ginger Boyer
Designed by April Ward

DEDICATIONS
AND/OR WEAKNESSES

FOR COUNT
DRACULA—
sunlight, garlic,
crosses,
sharp sticks

FOR
WOLFMAN—
silver,
wolfsbane

FOR AMANDA—
dander, chipotle,
credit-card
debt, phonies

FOR
SCOTT—
light beer

The
illustrator
would also like
to give thanks to
John James Audubon,
Richard Scarry, Maurice
Sendak, Edward Gorey,
Charles M. Schulz, and the
casts and crews of rather a lot
of motion pictures from the
last eighty-odd years. Probably
some other people as well.
To these people and their
descendants, he also
dedicates this book.

The Invisible Man Makes a Snow Angel, 1897

MENU

"FOOD GOOD"

W hen Frankenstein
prepared to dine
on ham-and-cheese on wheat,

he found, instead,
he had no bread
(or mustard, cheese, or meat).

What could he do?
He thought it through
until his brain was sore,

And thought he ought
to see what he could
borrow from next door.

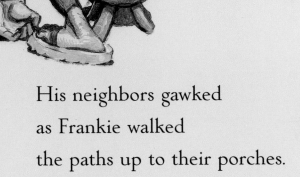

His neighbors gawked
as Frankie walked
the paths up to their porches.

Each time he tried,
the folks inside
would chase him off with torches.

"A MONSTER! EEK!"
the people shrieked.
"Oh, make him go away!"

The angry hordes
unsheathed their swords,
pulled pitchforks out of hay.

They threw tomatoes,
pigs, potatoes,
loaves of moldy bread.

And then a thought
struck Frankenstein
as pickles struck his head.

It's true, at first
he thought the worst:
His neighbors were so rude!

But then he found
that on the ground
they'd made a mound of *food.*

He piled it high
and waved good-bye
and shouted, **"Thanks a bunch!"**

Then stacked it on a plate and ate a big, disgusting lunch.

THE CREATURE FROM THE BLACK LAGOON

DOESN'T WAIT AN HOUR BEFORE SWIMMING

The Creature from the Black Lagoon
went back into the bog too soon.
"Too soon!" his doting mother cried.
"You just ate lunch! Come back inside!
That Black Lagoon is dark and damp.
You're going to get a stomach cramp!
Just think of all you had for lunch:
A squid! Three eels! Hawaiian Punch!
A bag of chips! A crab knish!
A peanut-butter jellyfish!
You have to wait an hour or more!"
she shouted from the kitchen door.
Alas, the creature never heard.
He hadn't listened to a word.
And rushing to
the water's bank,
he dived into
the dismal dank…

then gurgled,
got a cramp…
and sank.

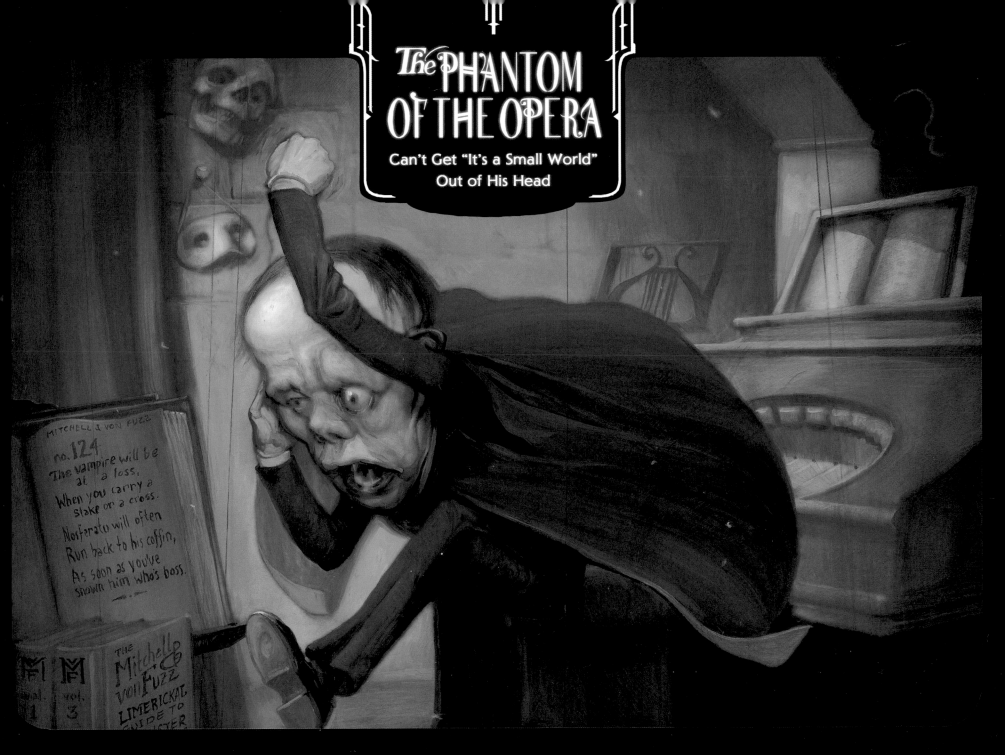

The PHANTOM OF THE OPERA

Can't Get "It's a Small World"
Out of His Head

It's a world gone crazy, a world gone wrong,
when the phantom can't even write a song.
Sure, he's using his head,
but what's stuck there instead?
"It's a Small World" after all.

It's a small world after all.
Angry cursing fills the hall.
Now he's crawling up the wall.
It's a small, small world.

THE MIDDLEWICH WITCH-WATCHERS CLUB:

A CLUB WHICH WATCHES WITCHES

Witch Watchers hide in trees and shrubs or settle deep in ditches.

And when they spot a witch, they look to see which witch it was.

They check inside the *Witch Watch Book* by Mitchell & von Fuzz.

PLATE I.

Today they saw a Speckled Crone, which shrieked while eating flies.

PLATE II.

And then a Frazzled Warthag, baking kid and kidney pies.

PLATE III.

The Long-Beaked Harpy
does this trick with eels
you've got to see.

(The Middlewich
Witch Watchers
spotted one
while having tea.)

When evening came and nighttime spilled its ink across the sky,
the Middlewich Witch Watchers packed their things and waved good-bye.
But then, by chance, they glanced upon the rarest witch of all:

PLATE IV.

A Ruby-Throated Cackler!
Look! Her hat is six feet tall!

Quiet, now, and listen to her sweet, alluring call:

Cackledy cack, and jiggedy jig!
Sit on a monkey and SNACK ON A PIG!
Hickory dickory cacklety coo!
Cack cack-a doodle-a DOOOOOOOOO!

12

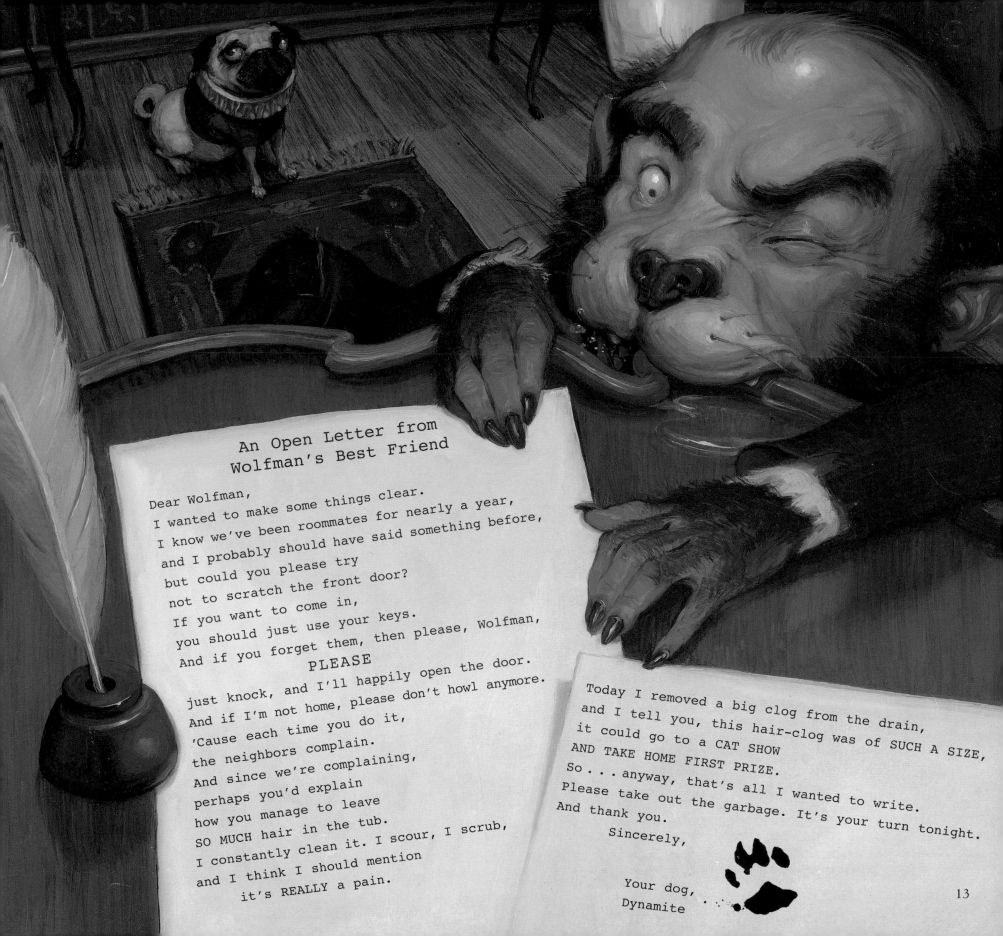

An Open Letter from
Wolfman's Best Friend

Dear Wolfman,
I wanted to make some things clear.
I know we've been roommates for nearly a year,
and I probably should have said something before,
but could you please try
not to scratch the front door?
If you want to come in,
you should just use your keys.
And if you forget them, then please, Wolfman,
PLEASE
just knock, and I'll happily open the door.
And if I'm not home, please don't howl anymore.
'Cause each time you do it,
the neighbors complain.
And since we're complaining,
perhaps you'd explain
how you manage to leave
SO MUCH hair in the tub.
I constantly clean it. I scour, I scrub,
and I think I should mention
it's REALLY a pain.

Today I removed a big clog from the drain,
and I tell you, this hair-clog was of SUCH A SIZE,
it could go to a CAT SHOW
AND TAKE HOME FIRST PRIZE.
So . . . anyway, that's all I wanted to write.
Please take out the garbage. It's your turn tonight.
And thank you.
    Sincerely,

        Your dog,
        Dynamite

13

THIS FIRST GUY, OF COURSE, GALLOPED UP ON A HORSE, AND HIS FACE FILLS THE BARBER WITH FEAR. HE HAS, NOT A HEAD, BUT A PUMPKIN INSTEAD, AND THE BARBER CAN'T TELL WHY HE'S HERE.

THE MAN NEXT TO HIM WANTS A SHAVE AND A TRIM, SO HE HAS TO BE SOME KIND OF NUT. THE FELLA'S A GHOST, SO HIS HAIR, AT THE MOST, CAN BE SEEN BUT NOT POSSIBLY CUT.

THE GAL AT THE DOOR HAS BEEN IN HERE BEFORE. HER HAIR ATE HIS BEST PAIR OF SHEARS

AND THE ONE IN THE CHAIR SAYS SHE'S SICK OF HER HAIR, AND SHE WANTS IT LIKE BRITNEY SPEARS.

14

THE INVISIBLE MAN
GETS A HAIRCUT

"My hair is a fright!"
said Griffin one night.
"At least I *assume* that it is.
It feels awfully long,
and the part is all wrong,
and it's knotted with tangles and frizz."

An invisible ne'er-do-well's hairdo will scare you,
no matter *how* well you cut hair.
The barber, downhearted,
took aim and got started.
The whole thing went downhill from there.

Said Griffin, "Oh my!
That's your thumb in my eye!
And my nostril's no place for a comb.
Oh dear! Where's my ear?
Well I know it was here
on my head when I checked it at home!"

He shouted, "Enough!
You are being too rough!"
Then Griffin jumped out of the chair.
So, Invisible Man
wears a visible hat
to conceal his invisible hair.

15

Count Dracula Doesn't Know He's Been Walking Around All Night with Spinach in His Teeth

Will someone please just tell him? It looks *so* undignified.
The zombies almost mentioned it. The Headless Horseman tried.
But when he said, "Vhat are you staring at?" they lost their nerve and lied.

It's been stuck in there for hours now. It's getting kind of sick.
I would offer him a toothpick, but he gets this nervous tic
if you ever come too close with any kind of pointed stick.

Well, really. Can you blame us if we don't know what to say?
His castle has no mirrors, so I guess it's there to stay.
What was a vampire doing eating spinach, anyway?

THE MUMMY WON'T GO TO HIS ETERNAL REST WITHOUT A STORY AND SOME COOKIES

There's a place in France
where the naked ladies dance.
But when King Tut died,
he wore bandages for pants.

〜〜〜〜〜〜〜〜〜〜

And he'll never, never go to sleep, no.
He will never, never go to sleep, oh!

⊙

"It is time for bed,"
all the royal servants said.
Mummy played on the floor,
and he wailed, "Five minutes more!"

〜〜〜〜〜〜〜〜〜〜

Here's his new excuse:
He wants cookies with his juice.
But he won't get far—
that's his stomach in that jar.

Now he wants to read,
so the scribes must do the deed.
They make groaning sounds,
'cause the books weigh thirty pounds.

And they said, "You're dead!
So you have to go to bed!"
But he runs through the tombs,
and he hides in secret rooms.

"Nyah nyah *nyaaaaah* nyah nyah,
nyah nyah nyah nyah nyah nyah nyah!"

The Yeti Doesn't Appreciate Being Called Bigfoot

Did you just say *Bigfoot?*
What's wrong with your eyes?
My feet aren't *remotely* as big as that guy's!
Nor are they as smelly.
You see, here's the truth:
Some folks call him Sasquatch.
His real name is Ruth,
so then why is Bigfoot
the name people mention?
The *smell,* not the *size,*
is what gets their attention.
His nose is big, too,
but does anyone care?
Perhaps if it smelled they
would be more aware.

Well . . . of course
his nose *smells,*
but . . . you know
what I meant.
You can bet
he's no Yeti
by way of his scent.

If **The PHANTOM OF THE OPERA** Can't Get "Pop Goes the Weasel" Out of His Head HE'S GOING TO FREAK OUT

All around the Opera House
the Phantom throws a tantrum.
The song won't die—he doesn't know why.
"Stop!" goes the phantom.

THE LUNCHSACK of NOTRE DAME

I'm stumped as to why we all lump this poor chump
with the rest of the monsters, just 'cause of his hump.
It's not like he drains all the blood from your veins,
or sucks out your brains and then eats your remains.

I bet when he packs all those brown paper sacks
and he takes them for lunch, breakfast, dinner, or brunch,
that he'll munch, snack, and chew on the same food as you.

Just a hunch.

DR. JEKYLL AND MR. HENDERSON

DR. H. JEKYLL

THE DOCTOR SIGHED, his tie was tied,
he fiddled with his combs.
He hated all these dressy balls
in crowded halls and homes.

He couldn't dance; he found that
fancy food just made him choke,
and guests would heckle Jekyll
if he tried to make a joke.

The clock began to chime,
the time was eight, and he was late.
He'd rather go to bed
instead of going out. But wait!

The notion of a certain potion
filled him with delight.
Why stay inside when Mr. Hyde
could go out for the night?

CONTINUED ON NEXT PAGE

MITCHELL & VON FUZZ CONTINUED FROM PAGE 22

If invisible men cause complaint,
get a squirt gun, and fill it with paint.
And wherever you go,
squirt around you to show
who's a visible man, and who ain't.

The following monsters require
the swift application of fire:
- Frankenstein
- mummy
- ventriloquist's dummy

Anyone who says different's a liar.

CONFIDENTIAL TO D. OF KANSAS:
Some witches don't melt when they're wet.
If you soak them they just get upset.
Try hard not to smirk,
or you'll look like a jerk,
and will likely deserve what you get.

MR. E. HYDE

Sure, Hyde was snide, he always lied,
and women cried to see him.
And yet, it still was such a thrill
when Jekyll got to be him.

You should see him dance the polka!
Fancy folk avoid his feet
as he reels and whirls the girls
around the hall and down the street.

He laughed and mixed the draft
that makes a gentleman a jerk,
and thought a lot about the ball,
but not about his work.

'Twas all his fault
he added salt,
instead of
crumbled skull.

FIG. 1

Salt

FIG. 2   FIG. 3

Skull   Crumbled Skull

The vial of bile
was pickle juice,
and dill
just made
it dull.

FIG. 4

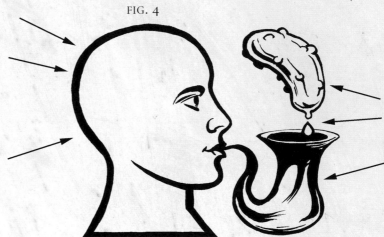

The Juicing of the Pickle, and Its Consequences

Alas, the glass of Cream of Evil
mixed with Powdered Creep
was really milk
the maid had laid
aside to help
him sleep.

FIG. 5

The Maid Swoons

He never knew. He drank the brew
while running out the door.
(Although he thought the beaker
tasted weaker than before.)

He reached the ball, and looked
in all the mirrors at his head.
It wasn't Hyde he spied inside,
but Henderson instead.

His shoulders stooped, his
eyelids drooped, his face
looked pooped and wan.
And where the hair of Hyde
was fried, this hair looked
plastered on.

"What's done . . . is done,"
sighed Henderson,
and went to join the rest.
Around the floor he stopped
to bore the pants off every guest.

MR. N. HENDERSON

He told a stale and endless tale
that tested their endurance,
topped that with pictures of his cat,
then sold them all insurance.

For Henderson possessed
one-tenth the zest
that Jekyll had.
Far less, in fact—he lacked
the personality of plaid.

The guests professed
they needed rest,
they had an early morning.
They couldn't stay;
they edged away, but then,
without a warning,

Their way was blocked,
the exit locked,
with Henderson ahead!
O cruel ennui! He held the key!
And wearily he said:

"You know... the sight of all you people trying to get away has made me mindful of a funny yarn I read the other day. And when I mention yarn... you know... I really mean to say I read a story—not a yarn in any woolly sort of way. Although I think we'd all agree that yarn is thrilling, eh? I'd listen to a yarn about some yarn most any day. Alas, that's not the funny yarn I'm trying to convey. (This tale is funny 'strange,' not funny 'ha-ha,' by the way). It seems a certain donkey living out in Santa Fe was made to toil the day away by pulling cargo in a dray. A dray's a sort of cart, you know. This one was filled with hay. But that's not really relevant. The thing I want to say is that this donkey in particular looked rather smart and gay—owing mostly to the fact he wore a polka-dot beret. And if any fellow tried to take the donkey's hat away, then the ass (that is, the donkey) would get very cross and neigh— Wait...horses neigh, not donkeys. What I mean to say is *bray*. He would bray, not neigh, if someone took his polka-dot beret. Which reminds me of an anecdote I heard my milkman say..."

(Zoo.)

Zombie? Zombie.

Zombie? ZOMBIE!

Samba!

Zombie Samba!

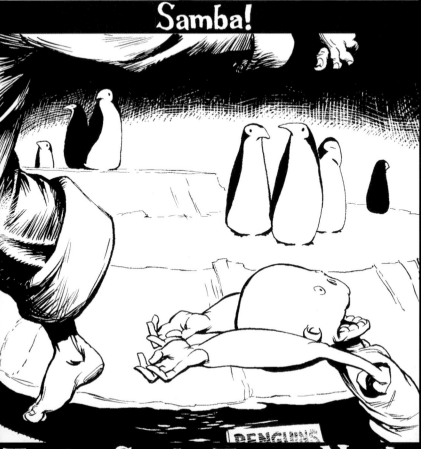

Zombie Samba Zombie Mamba

Mamba Mambo Zombie Zoo.

Rhumba Rhumba Zombie Samba

Zombie zimbie Bambi boo

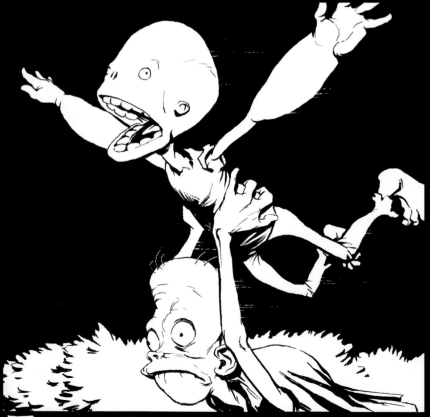

Zombie beeza bombie zamba

Bumba zumba Zombie—BEE!

BEE! BEE! BEE!

BEEEEEEEEEEEEEEEEE

CEEEEEEEEEEBump.

Zombie Zombie.

31

**Can't Get
"The Girl from Ipanema"
Out of His Head**

Bald and pale and masked and ugly, the Phantom of the Opera is writing, but when he knows that he can't compose he goes, "AAAHRG!"

Every song comes out a samba, although he wants to write an aria, so his top blows and he tears his clothes and goes, "AAAHRG!"

THE Dentist

Poor Son of Dracula. He's just a dud.
His daddy is famous, but *his* name is mud.
For how much blood
could a bloodsucker suck,
if a bloodsucker can't suck blood?

Ahem.

Everything's fine if he sucks on the throat
of a dog or a hog or a cat or a goat.
But a cold-blooded thing like a lizard or snake
makes his head start to hurt and his fangs really ache.

Frankenjunior was shocked. "You'll have to go see
the worst monster of all! She's much worse than me.
Her fingers are hooks! Hooks, needles, and spears!
Her voice is a high buzzing whine in your ears!
Instead of a head there's a BIG GLOWING EYE!"
The Frankenboy said with a shuddering sigh.

33

"She doesn't sound scary," said Dracula's son.
"Not scary like crosses, or stakes, or the sun."
So he made his appointment for just after dark
at the New Transylvania Medical Park.

"It's awful," he whispered. "So cheery and bright!
You'd think it would kill them to turn off a light.
They need some nice coffins. It's really a shame,"
young Dracula said as the nurse called his name.

He followed inside, and before he could hide,
the dentist was standing there, right by his side!
A note to the timid, or just faint of heart:
This story has come to the frightening part.
Stop reading! Now put the book down! This is scary!
Peligro! Use caution! Beware and be wary!

Still here? Very well. Little Drac stood in terror.
He knew now he'd made the most horrible error.
If he weren't undead he'd have wanted to die.
She was terrible! Awful! She smiled and said hi!

Her voice was a sweet lilting song in his ears.
Her fingers were fingers, not needles or spears.
That big glowing eye was a lamp, not a head.
It was all so much worse than The Frankenboy said!

Young Drac couldn't move, so she forced him to sit.
"Open wide, now," she told him. "This won't hurt a bit!"
"You aren't flossing," she scolded, and Dracula blushed.
"And honestly, when was the last time you brushed?
You really must brush after every bite.
See? A cavity's formed in this fang on the right."

"It needs to be mended. And so, if you're willing,
I'll patch it right up with a small silver filling."
A filling? With silver? Drac wanted to shout,
the werewolves will hate me! I've got to get out!

He changed to a bat—he flew up and away.
The dentist said, "Fine. We won't do it today.
"But get it fixed soon; you'll be glad that you did.
Now here—take a sucker. You've been a good kid."

He flew from the office, and homeward he raced.
He sucked on the sucker, but gagged at the taste.
He'd hoped it was flavored like blood, or like liver,
How scary! It's CHERRY! he thought with a shiver.

Drac knew it was true as he spat and he cursed,
My dad may be bad, but the dentist's THE WORST.

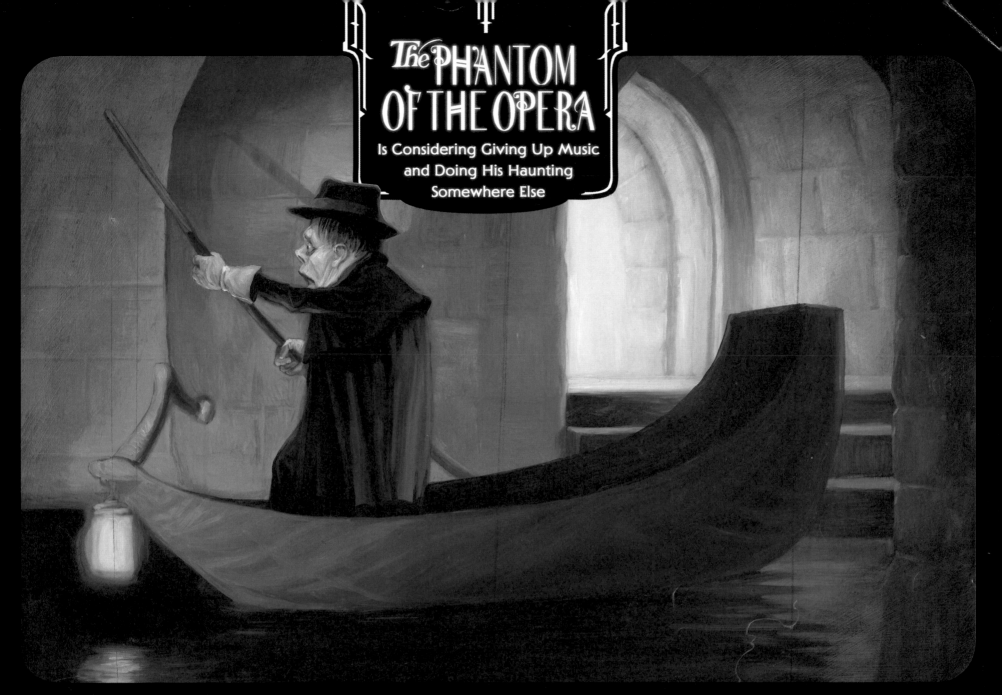

The PHANTOM OF THE OPERA

Is Considering Giving Up Music
and Doing His Haunting
Somewhere Else

There was a phantom
had a song,
and BINGO was its name-o.
B-I-N-G-O
See? I told you so.
B-I-N-G-O
By jingo! What a lame-o.

It bugged the phantom
all night long.
He never was the same-o.
(*clap*) His cheeks don't show,
(*clap*) if they *did*, though,
(*clap*) we'd see them glow
flamingo pink with shame-o.

At least the phantom
knows it's wrong.
It caused him to proclaim-o:
(*clap*) (*clap*) "I'll have no . . .
(*clap*) (*clap*) peace, and so . . .
(*clap*) (*clap*) I'll just go
and haunt a bingo game-o."

Bigfoot Can't Believe You Called Him Yeti Just Now

Wait, what did you say? The Yeti? No way!
I know that I'm going a little bit gray.
(Though I'm told all the time
I can still pass for thirty.)
But Yeti's all white! Except when he's dirty.
 And man, is he dirty. You might as well know:
  The Yeti is sweaty. *Despite* all the snow.
  They call him Abominable for a reason.
  That snowman's BO-man in every season.

Hey . . . sorry I shouted—
you gave me a fright.
You don't really think
we're *that* similar, right?

ゴジラ
が私のホンダにウンコした
(Godzilla Pooped on My Honda)

Don't ever go to Tokyo.
I just heard on the radio
that Ghidorah has taken wing
to fight some sort of turtle thing.
And as the monster flew away,
they saw a zipper, plain as day.
It seems perhaps these giant brutes
are giant men in suits.

I swear I'm leaving Tokyo.
I watched as, just a week ago,
some robots crushed my mailbox flat.
And only two days after that
a moth the size of Fuji goes
and chews up all my Sunday clothes.
I bought a mothball from the store.
It won't fit through the door.

And just last night, what did I see?
Turdzilla where my car should be.
It's not so bad—I'm sure some dupe
will pay for real Godzilla poop.
I'll make a sign—or better yet,
I'll sell it on the Internet!
And when I've made enough I'll go—
to any place but Tokyo.